Karim Benzema

Published by **Creative Education** and **Creative Paperbacks**
P.O. Box 227, Mankato, Minnesota 56002
Creative Education and Creative Paperbacks are imprints of
The Creative Company
www.thecreativecompany.us

Design and production by **Christine Vanderbeek**
Art direction by **Rita Marshall**
Printed in the United States of America

Photographs by Alamy (dpa picture alliance), Corbis (Manuel Blondeau,
Sandor Bojar/epa, epa, Stephane Mantey/TempSport, Mirrorpix/Splash
News, José Luis Morejón/Cordon Press, Visionhaus), Creative Commons
Wikimedia (El País), Getty Images (Simon Bruty, Pedro Castillo),
photosinbox.com, Shutterstock (anat chant, Rafael Ramirez Lee, tele52)

Library of Congress Cataloging-in-Publication Data
Whiting, Jim.
Real Madrid / Jim Whiting.
p. cm. — (Soccer stars)
Includes index.
Summary: An elementary introduction to the Spanish soccer team Real
Madrid, including a brief history since the team's 1902 founding, its main
rival, notable players, and Champions League titles.

ISBN 978-1-60818-804-8 (hardcover)
ISBN 978-1-62832-357-3 (pbk)
ISBN 978-1-56660-851-0 (eBook)
Real Madrid Club de Fútbol—History—Juvenile literature.
GV943.6.R35.W47 2016
796.3340946/41—dc23   2016000357

CCSS: RI.1.1, 2, 3, 4, 5, 6, 7; RI.2.1, 2, 4, 5, 6, 7, 10; RF.1.1, 3, 4; RF.2.3, 4

First Edition HC 9 8 7 6 5 4 3 2 1
First Edition PBK 9 8 7 6 5 4 3 2 1

Right: Keylor Navas

SOCCER STARS

REAL MADRID

Jim Whiting

CREATIVE EDUCATION • CREATIVE PAPERBACKS

Fernando Redondo

TABLE OF CONTENTS

Santiago spent most of his adult life with Real Madrid. After playing for Real as a striker, he became the manager (1936–41) and president (1943–78). The team's stadium was named after him in 1955.

Introducing Real Madrid

REAL (*RAY-ALL*) Madrid is one of the world's best teams. It plays in La Liga. La Liga is Spain's top soccer league.

Raúl González Blanco

REAL MADRID FAST FACTS

HOME ARENA: Estadio Santiago Bernabéu

Madrid, Spain

Madrid's Museums

THE TEAM IS based in Madrid, Spain's capital city. Madrid is home to three other La Liga teams. It is the biggest city in Spain. Many people visit Madrid's museums.

Francisco Román Alarcón Suárez (Isco)

TEAM COLORS: White, with black and blue or purple trim

The Classic

REAL'S RIVALRY with FC Barcelona is one of the most heated in sports. They have been rivals for more than 100 years! Their games are called *El Clásico* (the classic).

Madrid FC in 1905—06

Ricardo was a goalie known for wearing a cloth cap and white sweater during games. Today, the Ricardo Zamora Trophy is awarded to the best goalie in La Liga.

Royal Approval

MADRID FC WAS founded in 1902. In 1920, King Alfonso XIII let the team add the word *real* (royal) to its name. Real won its first two La Liga titles in 1932 and 1933. But then Spain fought a **civil war** from 1936 to 1939. *Los Blancos* did not play well for a long time after that.

14

SOCCER STARS   ALFREDO DI STÉFANO 1953–64

In 1999, Alfredo was voted fourth-best player of the 20th century. The forward scored 418 goals in 510 games with *Los Blancos*.

Real's Rise

IN 1953, Argentinian forward Alfredo Di Stéfano joined the team. He helped Real rise to the top again. Between 1953 and 1969, the team won La Liga 12 times! It also won the first five **Champions League** titles from 1956 to 1960.

David Beckham

SOCCER STARS   LUÍS FIGO 2000–05

Midfielder Luís joined *Los Blancos* after five years with FC Barcelona. Angry Barcelona fans threw chunks of brick, bicycle chains, fake money, and even a pig's head at Luís whenever he touched the ball.

Los Galácticos

THE TEAM won five titles in the 1970s, five more in the 1980s, and three in the 1990s. Real was nicknamed *Los Galácticos* early in the 2000s because it added star players such as David Beckham.

Cristiano Ronaldo

SOCCER STARS **CRISTIANO RONALDO 2009–present**

Soccer fans often **debate** whether Cristiano or FC Barcelona's Lionel Messi is the world's best player. In 2012, Cristiano became the first La Liga player to score a goal against every other team.

A Soccer Superpower

IN 2014, Real beat its hometown rival, Atlético Madrid, to win its 10th Champions League title. Superstars Cristiano Ronaldo, Gareth Bale, and Karim Benzema led the team to that win. Real Madrid fans look forward to many more titles in the coming years.

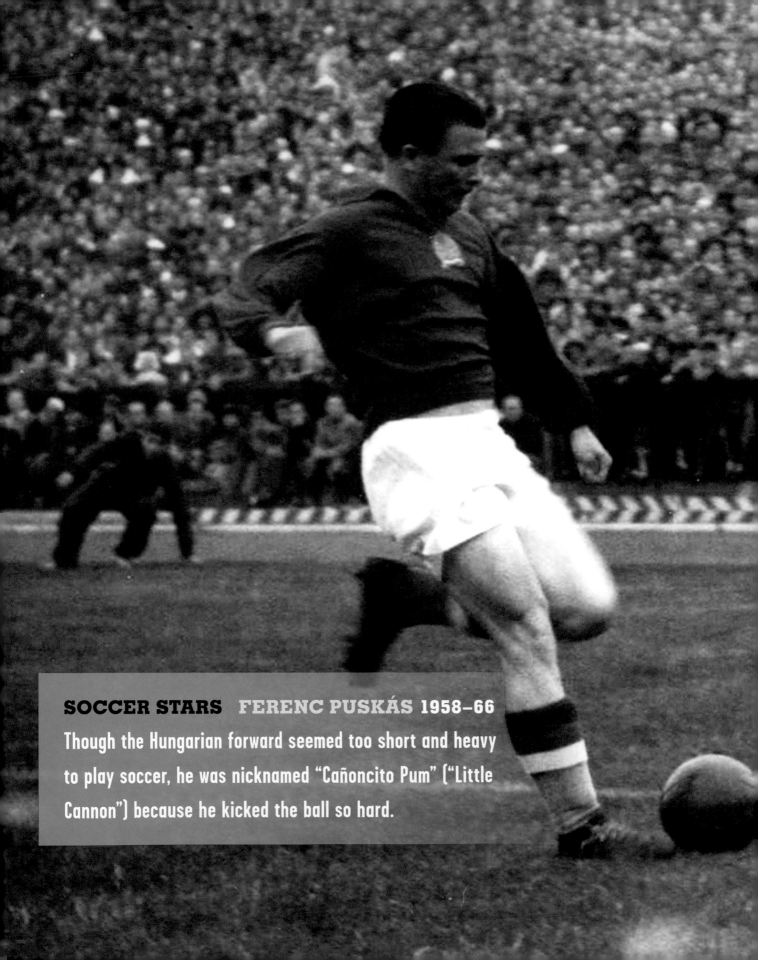

SOCCER STARS FERENC PUSKÁS 1958–66

Though the Hungarian forward seemed too short and heavy to play soccer, he was nicknamed "Cañoncito Pum" ("Little Cannon") because he kicked the ball so hard.

Champions League Titles

1956	Real Madrid	4
	Stade de Reims (France)	3
1957	Real Madrid	2
	Fiorentina (Italy)	0
1958	Real Madrid	3
	AC Milan (Italy)	2
1959	Real Madrid	2
	Stade de Reims (France)	0
1960	Real Madrid	7
	Eintracht Frankfurt (Germany)	3
1966	Real Madrid	2
	Partizan (Yugoslavia, now Serbia)	1
1998	Real Madrid	1
	Juventus (Italy)	0
2000	Real Madrid	3
	Valencia (Spain)	0
2002	Real Madrid	2
	Bayer Leverkusen (Germany)	1
2014	Real Madrid	4
	Atlético Madrid (Spain)	1

Read More

Jökulsson, Illugi. *Real Madrid: The Most Successful Club in the World*. New York: Abbeville Press, 2014.

Murray, Laura K. *Cristiano Ronaldo*. Mankato, Minn.: Creative Education, 2017.

Websites

REAL MADRID KID'S ZONE
http://www.realmadrid.com/en/fans/kids-zone
The official Real Madrid website for kids features links to games, *Hala Madrid Junior* magazine, and team information.

TOP 10 CHAMPIONS LEAGUE FINALS
http://www.sikids.com/photos/5201/top-10-champions-league-finals/1
Learn more about 10 notable Champions League finals matches.

Glossary

Champions League an annual tournament among the top European soccer teams to see which one is best

civil war a war between two or more groups in a country

debate to discuss or argue different sides of a topic

rivalry an intense competition between two teams

Note: Every effort has been made to ensure that the websites listed at left are suitable for children, that they have educational value, and that they contain no inappropriate material. However, because of the nature of the Internet, it is impossible to guarantee that these sites will remain active indefinitely or that their contents will not be altered.

Index